Big Sailor

My First Big ABC

Ages 3-5

Vol.8 V·W·X

Breadidu!
Your study buddy

My First Big ABC Book Series
Big Sailor Edu

Copyright © 2021 Cambridge Dynasty Press 𝕶

For permission requests, bulk order information, or any busine ss related inquries,
please contact the publisher at the email address below.

Cambridge Dynasty Press 𝕶
30 N Gould St. STE4000
Sheridan, WY 82801
Email: Bestsailoredu@Gmail.com

Written, Designed, and Printed in the United States of America

978-1-7357844-8-9(Paperback)

47678459

Hi! Nice to meet you.
My name is Breadidu!

I am your study buddy
for this book!

Let's work together on this book. We will get all of these amazing educational benefits!

1 Building Skills for Pen Control
2 Recognizing Alphabet Letters
3 Building Confidence
4 Enjoying a Good Book
5 Being Patient with Practice
6 Developing Creative Thinking
7 Being Proud of Achievement
8 Having Fun

This book belongs to

_____

(name)

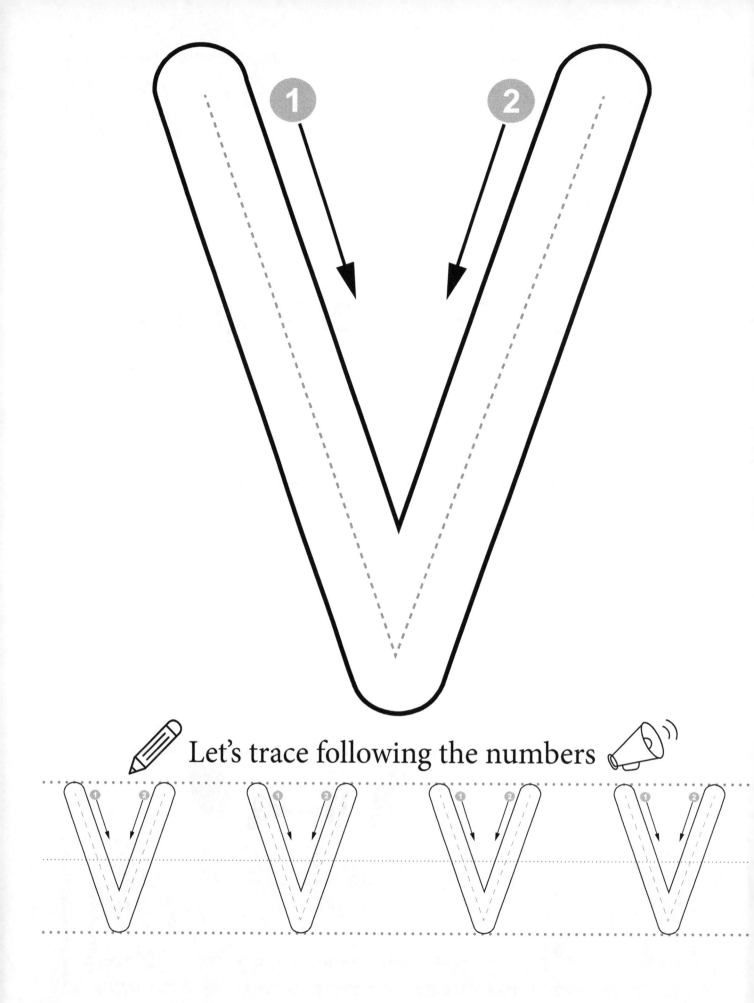

Let's trace following the numbers

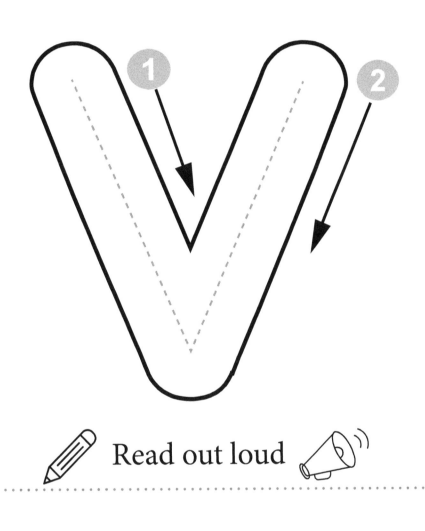

Read out loud

Van

 Let's trace following the numbers

V V V V

Vulture

vegetable

 Read out loud

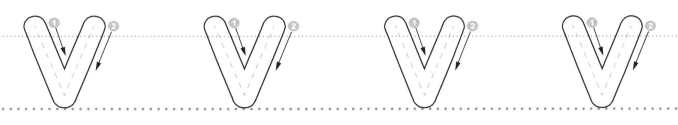

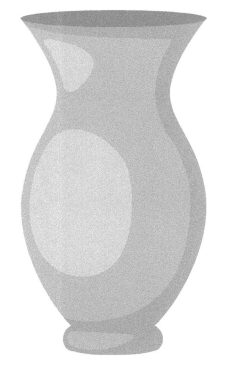 **vase**

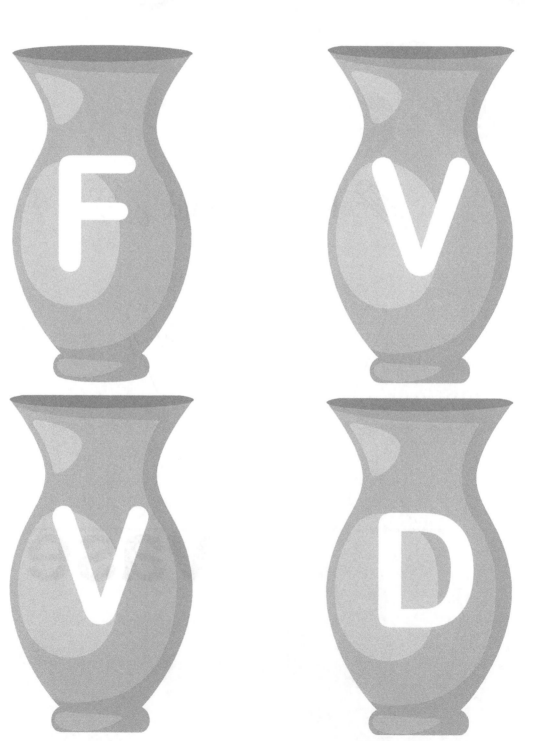

Trace the dotted line and read out loud

Find every V and color the sections

Breadidu

Find every v and circle them

t u v a v

o t e v m

d v s v k

v for van

Trace the dotted line and read out loud

V for Vegetable

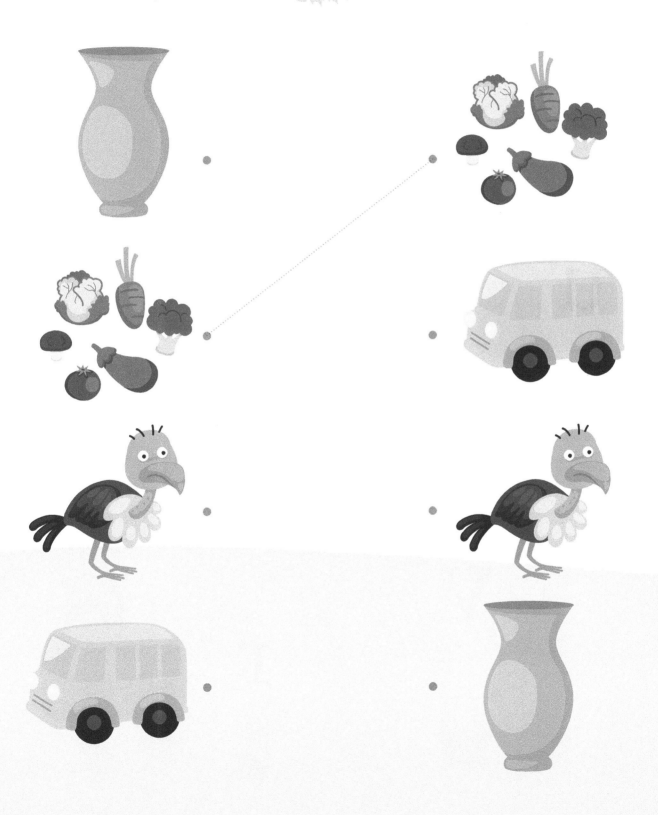

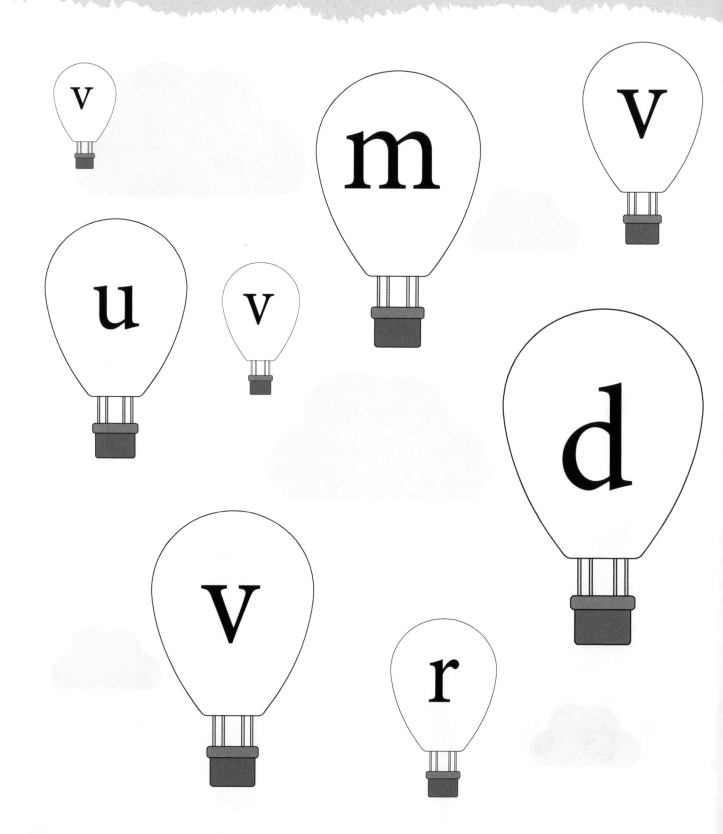

Trace the dotted line and read out loud

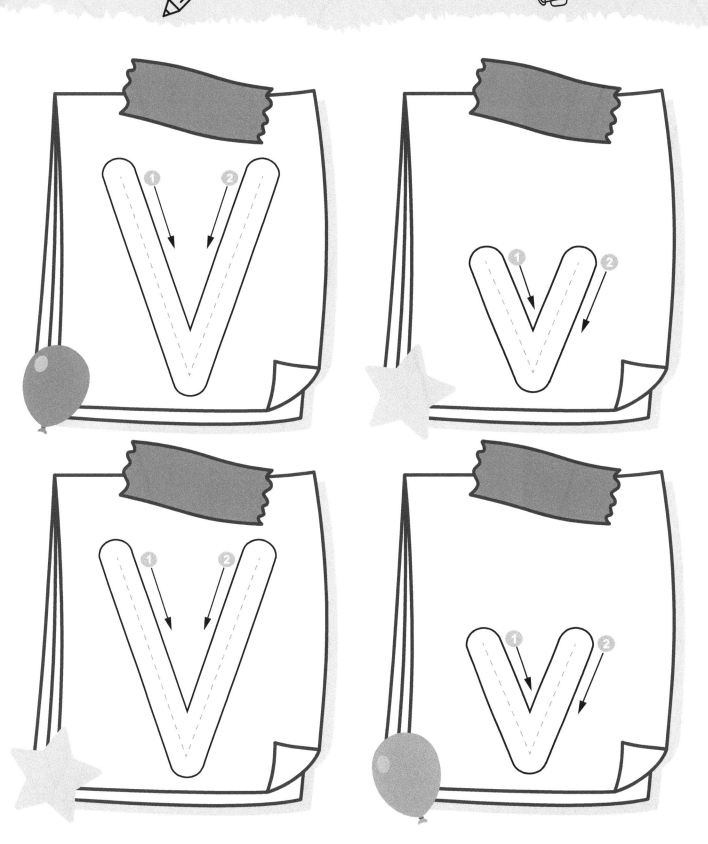

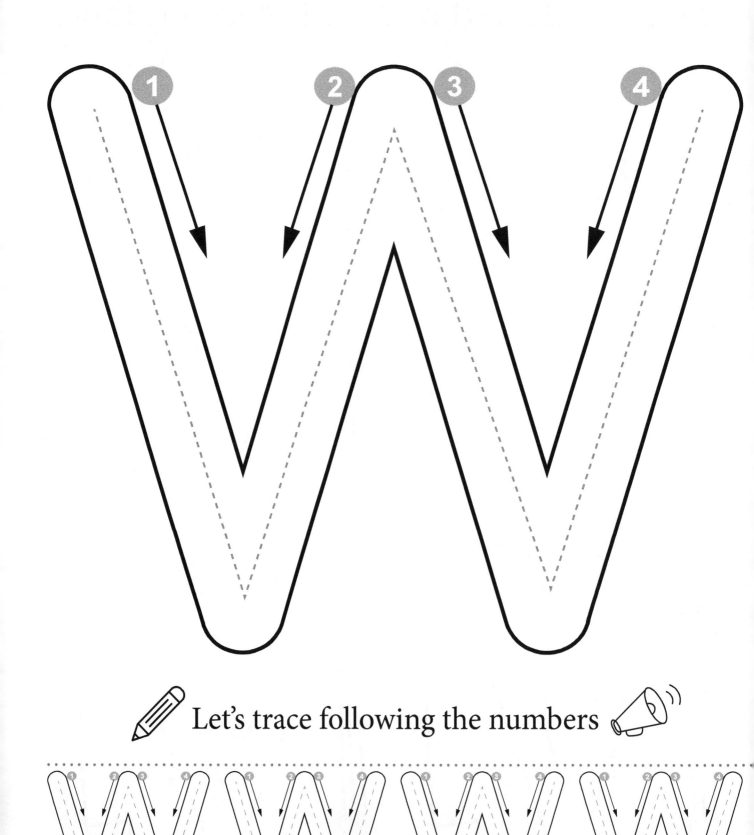

Let's trace following the numbers

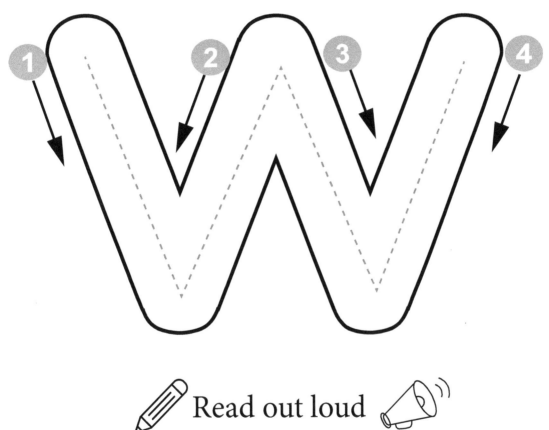

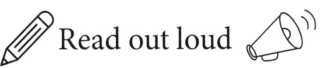 Read out loud

Whale

 Let's trace following the numbers

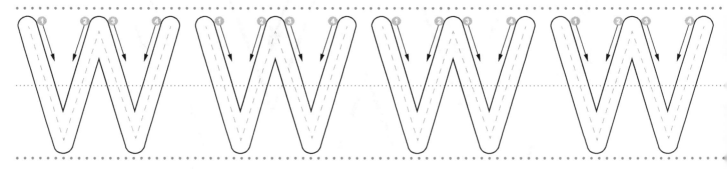

Wolf

worm

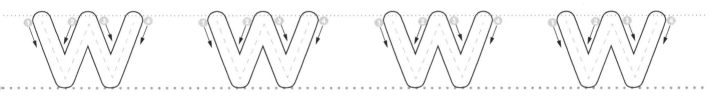

✏️ Read out loud 📢

 W W W W W

walrus

Find every W and color them

Trace the dotted line and read out loud

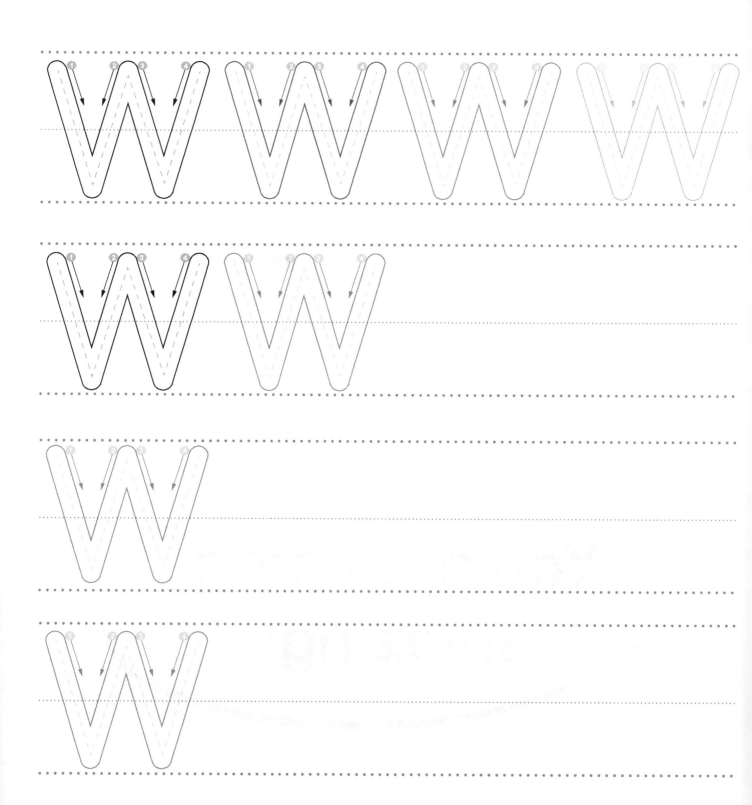

Breadidu

Find every w and circle them

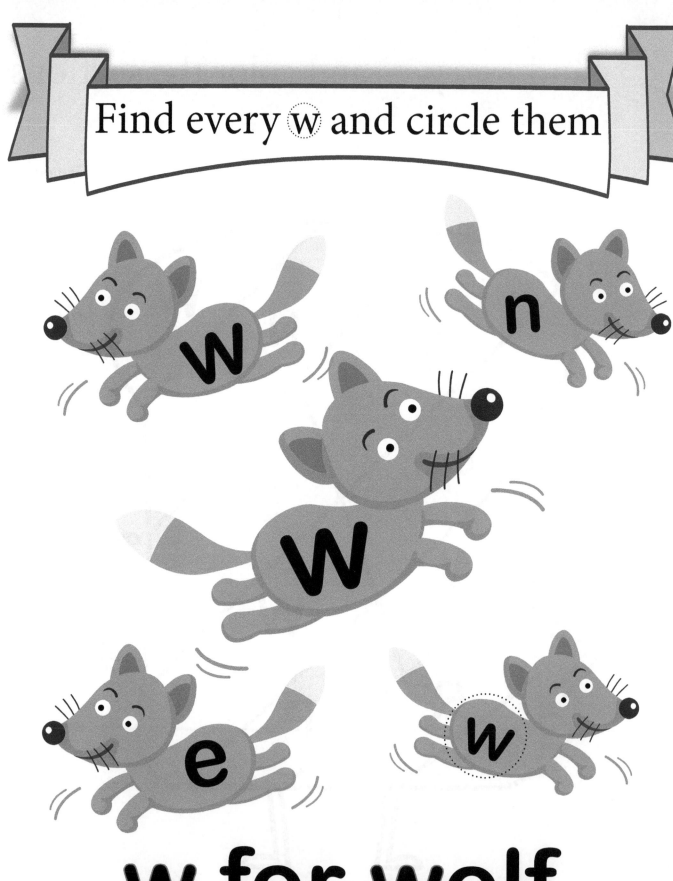

w for wolf

Trace the dotted line and read out loud

Draw lines to match

W for Whale

Find every W and color the sections

Trace the dotted line and read out loud

Let's trace following the numbers

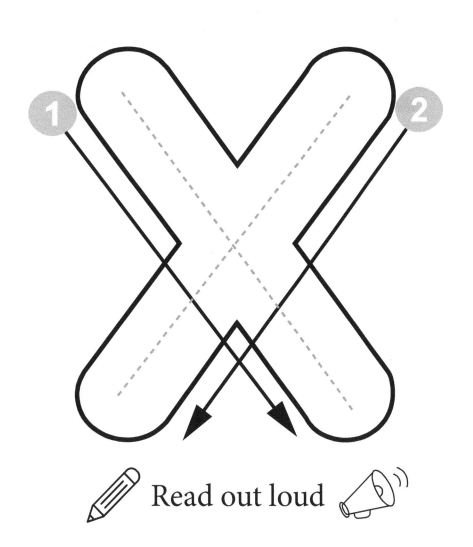

✏️ Read out loud 📢

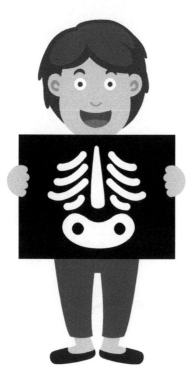

X-ray

 Let's trace following the numbers

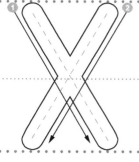 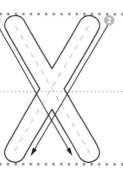 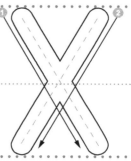 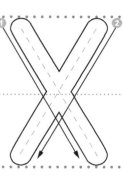

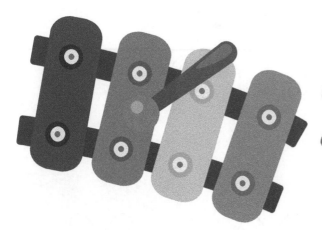 Xylophone

x-mas tree

✏️ Read out loud 📢

xiphias

Find every X and color them

Trace the dotted line and read out loud

Find every X and color the sections

Breadidu

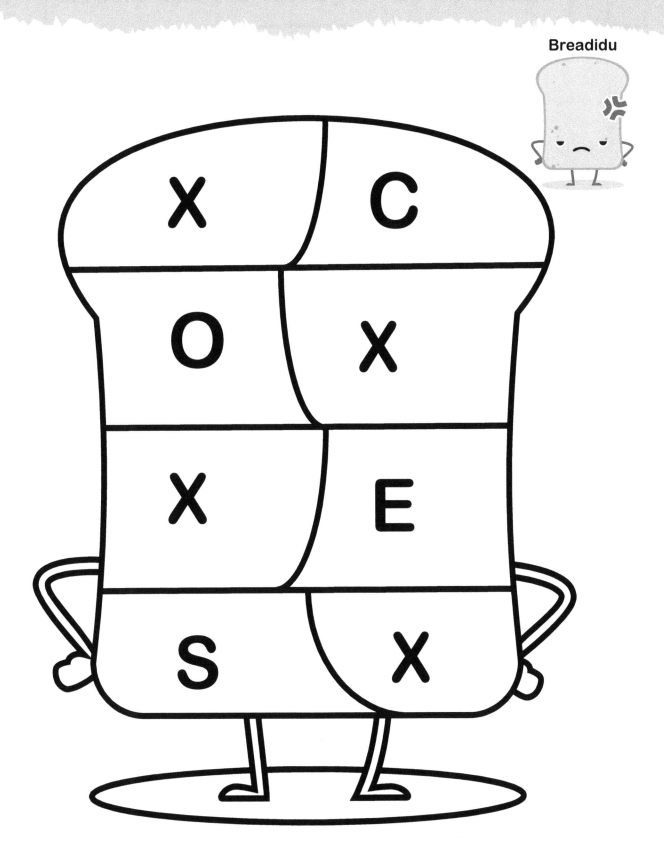

Find every x and circle them

x for xylophone

Trace the dotted line and read out loud

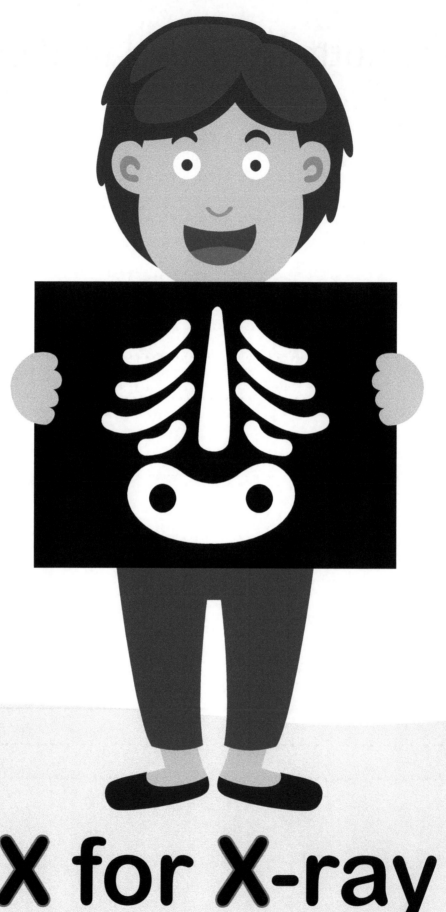

X for X-ray

Trace the dotted line and read out loud

Where is Breadidu?

Find and circle!

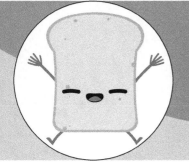

I am cool

I am hungry

I am playful

I am proud

I am okay

feelings with Breadidu!

I am tired

I am excited

I am loved

I am confident   I am happy

I am sad

I am calm

I am rushing

I am frustrated

I am angry

feelings with Breadidu!

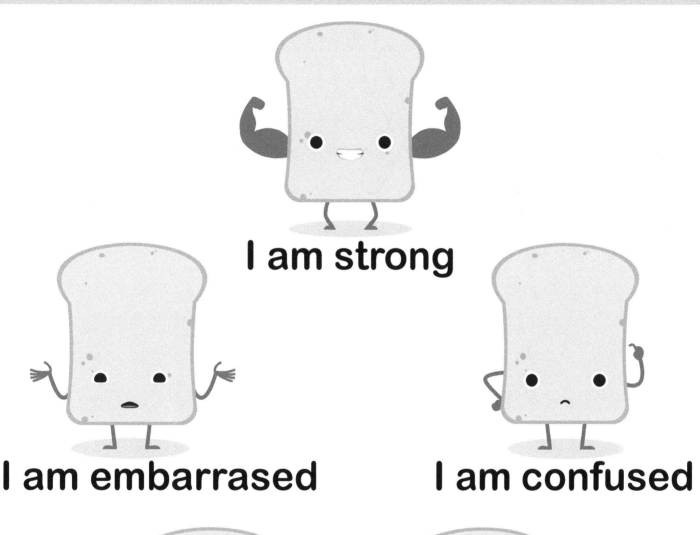

I am strong

I am embarrased

I am confused

I am shy

I am brave

Write VWX and read out loud

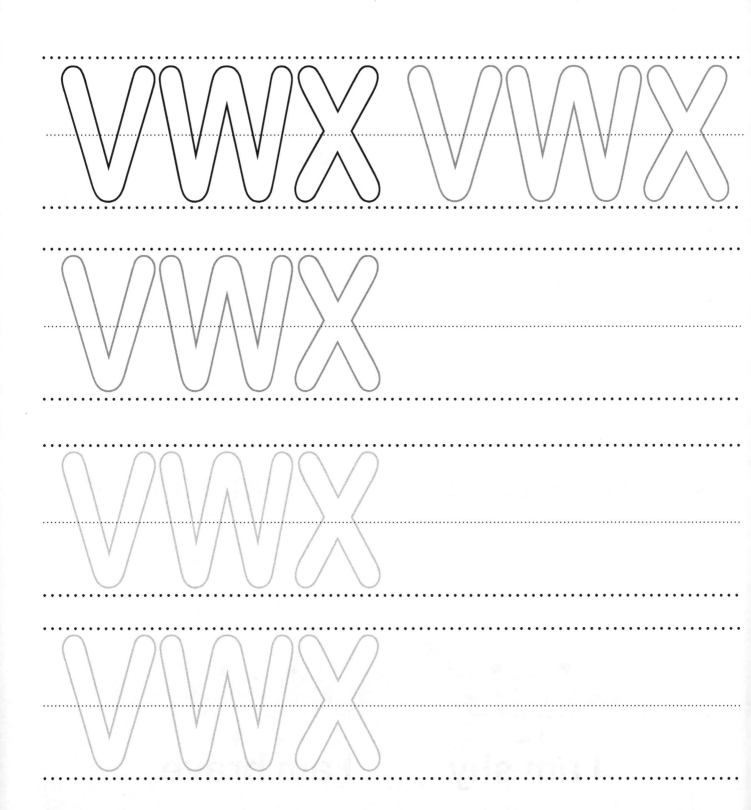

Write vwx and read out loud

Award

You are amazing!

This award is for

_____ _____
(first name)   (last name)

Great job finishing the book!

Date: _____

This award is for

_____

Great job finishing the book!

Date _____

Visit Our Website

BigSailorEdu.com

and Get Free & Fun

Educational Material

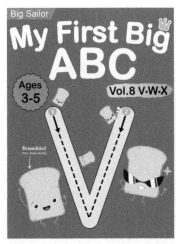

Cambridge Dynasty Press

CPSIA information can be obtained
at www.ICGtesting.com
Printed in the USA
BVHW012156111121
621433BV00004B/37